On the Origin of Money

By Carl Menger

Translated by Caroline Augusta Foley

Publisher's Note

BooksOfOld Reproduction Series: Our goal at BooksOfOld is to help readers, educators and researchers by bringing back hard-to-find original publications at a reasonable price and, at the same time, preserve the legacy of literary history. The following book represents an authentic reproduction of the text as printed by the original publisher and may contain prior copyright references. While we have attempted to accurately maintain the integrity of the original work(s), from time to time there are problems with the original book scan that may result in minor errors in the reproduction, including imperfections such as missing pages, poor pictures and other reproduction issues beyond our control. Because this work is culturally important, we have made it available as a part of our commitment to protecting, preserving and promoting the world's literature.

All of our books are in the "public domain" and some are derived from Open Source projects dedicated to digitizing historic literature. We believe that when we undertake the difficult task of re-creating them as attractive, readable and affordable books, we further the mutual goal of sharing these works with a larger audience.

ON THE ORIGIN OF MONEY.

I. Introduction

[239] THERE is a phenomenon which has from of old and in a peculiar degree attracted the attention of social philosophers and practical economists, the fact of certain commodities (these being in advanced civilizations coined pieces of gold and silver, together subsequently with documents representing those coins) becoming universally acceptable media of exchange. It is obvious even to the most ordinary intelligence, that a commodity should be given up by its owner in exchange for another more useful to him. But that every economic unit in a nation should be ready to exchange his goods for little metal disks apparently useless as such, or do documents representing the latter, is a procedure so opposed to the ordinary course of things, that we cannot well wonder if even a distinguished thinker like Savigny finds it downright "mysterious".

It must not be supposed that the *form* of coin, or document, employed as current-money, constitutes the enigma in this phenomenon. We may look away from these forms and go back to earlier stages of economic development, or indeed to what still obtains in countries here and there, where we find the precious metals in an uncoined state serving as the medium of exchange, and even certain other commodities, cattle, skins, cubes of tea, slabs of salt, cowrie-shells, etc.; still we are confronted by this phenomenon, still we have to explain why it is that the economic man is ready to accept a certain kind of commodity, *even if he does not need it, or if his need of it is already supplied*, in exchange for all the goods he has brought to the market, while it is none the less what he needs that he consults in the first instance, with respect to the goods he intends to acquire in the course of his transactions.

And hence there runs, from the first essays of reflective contemplation in social phenomena down to our own times, an uninterrupted chain of disquisitions upon the nature and specific qualities of money in its relation to all that constitutes traffic. Philosophers, jurists, and historians, as well as economists, and even naturalists and mathematicians, have dealt with this notable problem, and there is no civilized people that has not furnished its quota to the abundant literature thereon. What is the nature of those little disks or documents, which in themselves seem to serve no useful purpose, and which nevertheless, in contradiction to the rest of experience, pass from one hand to another in exchange for the most useful commodities, nay, for which every one is so eagerly bent on surrendering his wares? Is money an organic member in the world of commodities, or is it an economic anomaly? Are we to refer its commercial currency and its value in trade to the same causes conditioning those of other goods, or are they the distinct product of convention and authority?

II. Attempts at Solution Hitherto.

Thus far it can hardly be claimed for the results of investigation into the problem above stated, that they are commensurate either with the great development in historic research generally, or with the outlay of time and intellect expended in efforts at solution. The enigmatic phenomenon of money is even at this day without an explanation that satisfies; nor is there yet agreement on the most fundamental questions of its nature and functions. Even at this day we have no satisfactory theory of money.

The idea which lay first to hand for an explanation of the specific function of money as a universal current medium of exchange, was to refer it to a general convention, or a legal dispensation. The problem, which science has here to solve, consists in giving an explanation of a general, homogeneous course of action pursued by human beings when engaged in traffic, which, taken concretely, makes unquestionably for the common interest, and yet which seems to conflict with the nearest and immediate interests of contracting individuals. Under such circumstances what could lie more contiguous than the notion of referring the foregoing procedure to causes lying outside the sphere of individual considerations? To assume that certain commodities, the precious metals in particular, had been exalted [241] into the medium of exchange by general convention or law, in the interest of the commonweal, solved the difficulty, and solved it apparently the more easily and naturally inasmuch as the shape of the coins seemed to be a token of state regulation. Such in fact is the opinion of Plato, Aristotle, and the Roman jurists, closely followed by the mediaeval writers. Even the more modern developments in the theory of money have not in substance got beyond this standpoint.[1]

Tested more closely, the assumption underlying this theory gave room to grave doubts. An event of such high and universal significance and of notoriety so inevitable, as the establishment by law or convention of a universal medium of exchange, would certainly have been retained in the memory of man, the more certainly inasmuch as it would have had to be performed in a great number of places. Yet no historical monument gives us trustworthy tiding of any transactions either conferring distinct recognition on media of exchange already in use, or referring to their adoption by peoples of comparatively recent culture, much less testifying to an initiation of the earliest ages of economic civilization in the use of money.

And in fact the majority of theorists on this subject do not stop at the explanation of money as stated above. The peculiar adaptability of the precious metals for purposes of currency and coining was noticed by Aristotle, Xenophon, and Pliny, and to a far greater extent by John Law, Adam

---

[1] Cf. Roscher, *System der Volkswirthschaft*, I. § 116; my *Grundsätze der Volkswirtschaftslehre*, 1871, p. 255, *et seq.*; M. Block, *Les Progrès de la Science économique depuis A. Smith*, 1890, II., p. 59, *et seq.*

Smith and his disciples, who all seek a further explanation of the choice made of them as media of exchange, in their special qualifications. Nevertheless it is clear that the choice of the precious metals by law and convention, even if made in consequence of their peculiar adaptability for monetary purposes, presupposes the pragmatic origin of money, and selection of those metals, and that presupposition is unhistorical. Nor do even the theorists above mentioned honestly face the problem that is to be solved, to wit, the explaining how it has come to pass that certain commodities (the precious metals at certain stages of culture) should be promoted amongst the mass of all other commodities, and accepted as the generally acknowledged media of exchange. It is a question concerning not only the origin but also the nature of money and its position in relation to all other commodities.

III. The Problem of the Genesis of a Medium of Exchange.

[242] In primitive traffic the economic man is awaking but very gradually to an understanding of the economic advantages to be gained by exploitation of existing opportunities of exchange. His aims are directed first and foremost, in accordance with the simplicity of all primitive culture, only at what lies first to hand. And only in that proportion does the value in use of the commodities he seeks

to acquire, come into account in his bargaining. Under such conditions each man is intent to get by way of exchange just such goods as he directly needs, and to reject those of which he has no need at all, or with which he is already sufficiently provided. It is clear then, that in these circumstances the number of bargains actually concluded must lie within very narrow limits. Consider how seldom it is the case, that a commodity owned by somebody is of less value in use than another commodity owned by somebody else! And for the latter just the opposite relation is the case. But how much more seldom does it happen that these two bodies meet! Think, indeed, of the peculiar difficulties obstructing the immediate barter of goods in those cases, where supply and demand do not quantitatively coincide; where, *e.g.*, an indivisible commodity is to be exchanged for a variety of goods in the possession of different persons, or indeed for such commodities as are only in demand at different times and can be supplied only by different persons! Even in the relatively simple and so often recurring case, where an economic unit, A, requires a commodity possessed by B, and B requires one possessed by C, while C wants one that is owned by A—even here, under a rule of mere barter, the exchange of the goods in question would as a rule be of necessity left undone.

These difficulties would have proved absolutely insurmountable obstacles to the progress of traffic, and at the same time to the production of goods not commanding a regular sale, had there not lain a remedy in the very nature of things, to wit, *the different degrees of saleableness (Absatzfähigkeit) of commodities.* The difference existing in this respect between articles of commerce is of the highest degree of significance for the theory of money, and of the market in general. And the failure to turn it adequately to account in explaining the phenomena of trade, constitutes not only as such a lamentable breach in our science, [243] but also one of the essential causes of the backward state of monetary theory. *The theory of money necessarily presupposes a theory of the saleableness of goods.* If we grasp this, we shall be able to understand how the almost unlimited saleableness of money is only a special case,—presenting only a difference of degree—of a generic phenomenon of economic life—namely, the difference in the saleableness of commodities in general.

IV. COMMODITIES AS MORE OR LESS SALEABLE.

It is an error in economics, as prevalent as it is patent, that all commodities, at a definite point of time and in a given market, may be assumed to stand to each other in a definite relation of exchange, in other words, may be mutually exchanged in definite quantities at will. It is not true that in any given market 10 cwt. of an article = 2 cwt. of another = 3 lbs. of a third article, and so on. The most cursory observation of market-phenomena teaches us that it does not lie within our power, when we have bought an article for a certain price, to sell it again forthwith at the same price. If we but try to dispose of an article of clothing, a book, or a work of art, which we have just purchased, in the very same market, even though it be at once, before the same juncture of conditions has altered, we shall easily convince ourselves of the fallaciousness of such an assumption. The price at which any one can at pleasure buy a commodity at a given market and a given point of time, and the price at which he can dispose of the same at pleasure, are two essentially different magnitudes. This holds good of wholesale as well as retail prices. Even such marketable goods as corn, cotton, pig-iron, cannot be voluntarily disposed of for the price at which we have purchased them. Commerce and speculation would be the simplest things in the world, if the theory of the 'objective equivalent in goods' were correct, if it were actually true, that in a given market and at a given moment commodities could be mutually converted at will in definite quantitative relations—could, in short, at a certain price be as easily disposed of as acquired. At any rate there is no such thing as a general saleableness of wares in this sense. The truth is, that even in the best organized markets, while we may be able to purchase when and what we like at a definite price, viz.: the *purchasing price*, we can only dispose [244] of it again when and as we like at a loss, viz.: at the *selling price*.[1]

---

[1] We must make a distinction between the higher purchasing prices for which the buyer is rendered liable through the wish to purchase at a definite point of time, and the (lower) selling prices, which he, who is obliged to get rid

The loss experienced by any one who is compelled to dispose of an article at a definite moment, as compared with the current purchasing prices, is a highly variable quantity, as a glance at trade and at markets of specific commodities will show. If corn or cotton is to be disposed of at an organized market, the seller will be in a position to do so in practically any quantity, at any time he pleases, at the current price, or at most with a loss of only a few pence on the total sum. If it be a question of disposing, in larger quantities, of cloth or silk-stuffs at will, the seller will regularly have to content himself with a considerable percentage of diminution in the price. Far worse is the case of one who at a certain point of time has to get rid of astronomical instruments, anatomical preparations, Sanskrit writings, and such hardly marketable articles!

If we call any goods or wares *more or less saleable*, according to the greater or less facility with which they can be disposed of at a market at any convenient time at current purchasing prices, or with less or more diminution of the same, we can see by what has been said, that an obvious difference exists in this connection between commodities. Nevertheless, and in spite of its great practical significance, it cannot be said that this phenomenon has been much taken into account in economic science. The reason of this is in part the circumstance, that investigation into the phenomena

---

of goods within a definite period, must content himself withal. The smaller the difference between the buying and selling prices of an article, the more saleable it usually proves to be.

of price has been directed almost exclusively to the *quantities* of the commodities exchanged, and not as well to the greater or less *facility* with which wares may be disposed of at normal prices. In part also the reason is the thorough-going abstract method by which the saleableness of goods has been treated, without due regard to all circumstances of the case.

The man who goes to market with his wares intends as a rule to dispose of them, by no means at any price whatever, but at such as corresponds to the general economic situation. If we are going to inquire into the different degrees of saleableness in goods so as to show its bearing upon practical life, we can only do so by consulting the greater or less facility with which they may be disposed of at prices corresponding to the general economic [245] situation, that is, at *economic* prices.[1] A commodity is more or less saleable according as we are able, with more or less prospect of success, to dispose of it at prices corresponding to the general economic situation, at *economic* prices.

---

[1] The height of saleableness in a commodity is not revealed by the fact that it may be disposed of at any price whatever, including such as result from distress or accident. In this sense all commodities are pretty well equally saleable. A high rate of saleableness in a commodity consists in the fact that it may at every moment be easily and surely disposed of at a price corresponding to, or at least not discrepant from, the general economic situation—at the economic, or approximately economic price.

The price of a commodity may be denoted as *uneconomic* on two grounds: (1) in consequence of error, ignorance, caprice, and so forth; (2) in consequence of the circumstance that only a part of the supply is available to the demand, the rest for some reason or other being withheld, and the price in consequence not commensurate with the actually existing economic situation.

The *interval of time*, moreover, within which the disposal of a commodity at the economic price may be reckoned on, is of great significance in an inquiry into its degree of saleableness. It matters not whether the demand for a commodity be slight, or whether on other grounds its saleableness be small; if its owner can only bide his time, he will finally and in the long run be able to dispose of it at economic prices. Since, however, this condition is often absent in the actual course of business, there arises for practical purposes an important difference between those commodities, on the one hand, which we expect to dispose of at any given time at economic, or at least approximately economic, prices, and such goods, on the other hand, respecting which we have no such prospect, or at least not in the same degree, and to dispose of which at economic prices the owner foresees it will be necessary to wait for a longer or shorter period, or else to put up with a more or less sensible abatement in the price.

Again, account must be taken of the *quantitative* factor in the saleableness of commodities. Some commodities, in consequence of the development of markets and speculation, are able at any time to find a sale in practically any quantity at economic, or approximately economic, prices. Other commodities can only find a sale at economic prices in smaller quantities, commensurate with the gradual growth of an effective demand, fetching a relatively reduces price in the case of a greater supply.

V. Concerning the Causes of the Different Degrees of Saleableness in Commodities.

[246] The degree to which a commodity is found by experience to command a sale, at a given market, at any time, at prices corresponding to the economic situation (economic prices), depends upon the following circumstances.

1. Upon the number of persons who are still in want of the commodity in question, and upon the extent and intensity of that want, which is unsupplied, or is constantly recurring.

2. Upon the purchasing power of those persons.

3. Upon the available quantity of the commodity in relation to the yet unsupplied (total) want of it.

4. Upon the divisibility of the commodity, and any other ways in which it may be adjusted to the needs of individual customers.

5. Upon the development of the market, and of speculation in particular. And finally,

6. Upon the number and nature of the limitations imposed politically and socially upon exchange and consumption with respect to the commodity in question.

We may proceed, in the same way in which we considered the degree of the saleableness in commodities at definite markets and definite points of time, to set out the *spatial and temporal limits* of their saleableness. In these respects also we observe in our markets some commodities, the saleableness of which is almost unlimited by place or time, and others the sale of which is more or less limited.

The *spatial* limits of the saleableness of commodities are mainly conditioned—

1. By the degree to which the want of the commodities are distributed in space.

2. By the degree to which the goods lend themselves to transport, and the cost of transport incurred in proportion to their value.

3. By the extent to which the means of transport and of commerce generally are developed with respect to different classes of commodities.

4. By the local extension of organized markets and their intercommunication by 'arbitrage.'

5. By the differences in the restrictions imposed upon commercial intercommunication with respect to different goods, in interlocal and, in particular, in international trade.

[247] The time-limits to saleableness of commodities are mainly conditioned—

1. By permanence in the need of them (their independence of fluctuation in the same).

2. Their durability, *i.e.* their suitableness for preservation.

3. The cost of preserving and storing them.

4. The rate of interest.

5. The periodicity of a market for the same.

6. The development of speculation and in particular of time-bargains in connection with the same.

7. The restrictions imposed politically and socially on their being transferred from one period of time to another.

All these circumstances, on which depend the different degrees of, and the different local and temporal limits to, the saleableness of commodities, explain why it is that certain commodities can be disposed of with ease and certainty in definite markets, *i. e.* within local and temporal limits, at any time and in practically any quantities, at prices corresponding to the general economic situation, while the saleableness of other commodities is confined within narrow spatial, and again, temporal, limits; and even within these the disposal of the commodities in question is difficult, and, in so far as the demand cannot be waited for, is not to be brought about without a more or less sensible diminution in price.

VI. On the Genesis of Media of Exchange[1]

It has long been the subject of universal remark in centres of exchange, that for certain commodities there existed a greater, more constant, and more effective demand than for other commodities less desirable in certain respects, the former being such as correspond to a want on the part of

---

[1] *Cf.* my article 'Money' in the *Handwörterbuch der Staatswissenschaften* (Dictionary of Social Science), Jena, 1891, iii., p. 730 *et seq.*

those able and willing to traffic, which is at once universal and, by reason of the relative scarcity of the goods in question, always imperfectly satisfied. And further, that the person who wishes to acquire certain definite goods in exchange for his own is in a more favourable position, if he brings commodities of this kind to market, than if he visits the market with goods which cannot display such advantages, or at least not in the same degree. Thus equipped [248] he has the prospect of acquiring such goods as he finally wishes to obtain, not only with greater ease and security, but also, by reason of the steadier and more prevailing demand for his own commodities, at prices corresponding to the general economic situation—at economic prices. Under these circumstances, when any one has brought goods not highly saleable to market, the idea uppermost in his mind is to exchange them, not only for such as he happens to be in need of, but, if this cannot be effected directly, for other goods also, which, while he did not want them himself, were nevertheless more saleable than his own. By so doing he certainly does not attain at once the final object of his trafficking, to wit, the acquisition of goods needful to *himself.* Yet he draws nearer to that object. By the devious way of a mediate exchange, he gains the prospect of accomplishing his purpose more surely and economically than if he had confined himself to direct exchange. Now in point of fact this seems everywhere to have been the case. Men have been led, with increasing knowledge of their individual interests, each by his own economic interests, without convention, without legal compulsion, nay, even without any regard to the common interest, to exchange goods destined for exchange (their "wares") for other goods equally destined for exchange, but more saleable.

With the extension of traffic in space and with the expansion over ever longer intervals of time of prevision for satisfying material needs, each individual would learn, from his own economic interests, to take good heed that he bartered his less saleable goods for those special commodities which displayed, beside the attraction of being highly saleable in the particular locality, a wide range of saleableness both in time and place. These wares would be qualified by their costliness, easy transportability, and fitness for preservation (in connection with the circumstance of their corresponding to a steady and widely distributed demand), to ensure to the possessor a power, not only 'here' and 'now,' but as nearly as possible unlimited in space and time generally, over all other market-goods at economic prices.

And so it has come to pass, that as man became increasingly conversant with these economic advantages, mainly by an insight become traditional, and by the habit of economic action, those commodities, which relatively to both space and time are most saleable, have in every market become the wares, which it is not only in the interest of every one to accept in exchange for his own less saleable goods, but which also are those he actually does readily accept. And their superior saleableness depends only upon the relatively inferior saleableness of every other kind of [249] commodity, by which alone they have been able to become *generally* acceptable media of exchange.

It is obvious how highly significant a factor is habit in the genesis of such generally serviceable means of exchange. It lies in the economic interests of each trafficking individual to exchange less saleable for more saleable commodities. But the willing acceptance of the medium of exchange presupposes already a knowledge of these interests on the part of those economic subjects who are expected to accept in exchange for their wares a commodity which in and by itself is perhaps entirely useless to them. It is certain that this knowledge never arises in every part of a nation at the same time. It is only in the first instance a limited number of economic subjects who will recognize the advantage in such procedure, an advantage which, in and by itself, is independent of the general recognition of a commodity as a medium of exchange, inasmuch as such an exchange, always and under all circumstances, brings the economic unit a good deal nearer to his goal, to the acquisition of useful things of which he really stands in need. But it is admitted, that there is no better method of enlightening any one about his economic interests than that he perceives the economic success of those who use the right means to secure their own. Hence it is also clear that nothing may have been so favourable to the genesis of a medium of exchange as the acceptance, on the part of the most discerning and capable economic subjects, for their own economic gain, and over a considerable period of time, of eminently saleable goods in preference to all others. In this way practice and habit have certainly contributed not a little to cause goods, which were most saleable at any time to be accepted not only by many, but finally by all, economic subjects in exchange for their less saleable goods: and not only so, but to be accepted from the first with the intention of exchanging them away again. Goods which had thus become generally acceptable media of exchange were called by the Germans *Geld*, from *gelten, i.e.* to pay, to perform, while other nations derived their designation for money mainly from the substance used,[1] the shape of the coin,[2] or even from certain kinds of coin.[3]

[250] It is not impossible for media of exchange, serving as they do the commonweal in the most emphatic sense of the word, to be instituted also by way of legislation, like other social institutions. But this is neither the only, nor the primary mode in which money has taken its origin. Thhis is much more to be traced in the process depicted above, notwithstanding the nature of that process would be but very incompletely explained if we were to call it 'organic,' or

---

[1] The Hebrew *Keseph*, the Greek ἀργυρος, the Latin *argentum*, the French *argent*, etc.

[2] The English *money*, the Spanish *moneda*, the Portuguese *moeda*, the French *monnaie*, the Hebrew *maoth*, the Arabic *fulus*, etc.

[3] The Italien *danaro*, the Russian *dengi*, the Polish *pienondze*, the Bohemian and Slavonian *penize*, the Danish *penge*, the Swedish *penningar*, the Magyar *penz*, etc. (*i.e. denare = Pfennige = penny*).

denote money as something 'primordial,' of 'primaeval growth,' and so forth. Putting aside assumptions which are historically unsound, we can only come fully to understand the origin of money by learning to view the establishment of the social procedure, with which we are dealing, as the spontaneaous outcome, the unpremeditated resultant, of particular, individual efforts of the members of a society, who have little by little worked their way to a discrimination of the different degrees of saleableness in commodities.[1]

VII. The Process of Differentiation Between Commodities Which Have Become Media of Exchange and the Rest.

When the relatively most saleable commodities have become 'money,' the event has in the first place the effect of substantially increasing their originally high saleableness. Every economic subject bringing less saleable wares to market, to acquire goods of another sort, has thenceforth a stronger interest in converting what he has in the first instance into wares which have become money. For such persons, by the exchange of their less saleable wares for those which as money are most saleable, attain not merely, as heretofore, a higher probability, but the certainty, of being able to acquire forthwith equivalent quantities of every other kind of commodity to be had in the market. And their

---

[1] *Cf.* on this point my *Grundsätze der Volkswirtschaftslehre*, 1871, p. 250 *et seq.*

control over these depends simply upon their pleasure and their choice. *Pecuniam habens, habet omnem remquem vult habere.*

On the other hand, he who brings other wares than money to market, finds himself at a disadvantage more or less. To gain the same command over what the market affords, he must first convert his exchangeable goods into money. The nature of his economic disability is shown by the fact of his being compelled to overcome a difficulty before he can attain his purpose, which difficulty does not exist for, *i.e.* has already been overcome by, the man who owns a stock of money.

[251] This has all the greater significance for practical life, inasmuch as to overcome this difficulty does not lie unconditionally within reach of him who brings less saleable goods to market, but depends in part upon circumstances over which the individual bargainer has no control. The less saleable are his wares, the more certainly will he have either to suffer the penalty in the economic price, or to content himself with awaiting the moment, when it will be possible for him to effect a conversion at economic prices. He who is desirous, in an era of monetary economy, to exchange goods of any kind whatever, which are not money, for other goods supplied in the market, cannot be certain of attaining this result at once, or within any predetermined interval of time, at economic prices. And the less saleable are the goods brought by an economic subject to market, the more unfavourable, for his own purposes, will his economic

position compare with the position of those who bring money to market. Consider, *e.g.*, the owner of a stock of surgical instruments, who is obliged through sudden distress, or through pressure from creditors, to convert it into money. The prices which it will fetch will be highly accidental, nay, the goods being of such limited saleableness, they will be fairly incalculable. And this holds good of all kinds of conversions which in respect of time are compulsory sales.[1] Other is his case who wants at a market to convert the commodity, which has become *money*, forthwith into other goods supplied at that market. He will accomplish his purpose, not only with certainty, but usually also at a price corresponding to the general economic situation. Nay, the habit of economic action had made us so sure of being able to procure in return for money any goods on the market, whenever we wish, at prices corresponding to the economic situation, that we are for the most part unconscious of how many purchases we daily propose to make, which, with respect to our wants and the time of concluding them, are compulsory purchases. Compulsory sales, on the other hand, in consequence of the economic disadvantage which they commonly involve, force themselves upon the attention of the parties implicated in unmistakable fashion. What

---

[1] Herein lies the explanation of the circumstance why compulsory sales, and cases of distraint in particular, involve as a rule the economic ruin of the person upon whose estate they are carried out, and that in a greater degree the less the goods in question are saleable. Correct discernment of the uneconomic character of these processes will necessarily lead to a reform in the available legal mechanism.

therefore constitutes the particularity of a commodity which has become money is, that the possession of it procures for us at any time, *i.e.* [252] at any moment we think fit, assured control over every commodity to be had on the market, and this usually at prices adjusted to the economic situation of the moment: the control, on the other hand, conferred by other kinds of commodities over market goods is, in respect of time, and in part of price as well, uncertain, relatively if not absolutely.

Thus the effect produces by such goods as are relatively most saleable becoming money is an increasing differentiation between their degree of saleableness and that of all other goods. And this difference in saleableness ceases to be altogether gradual, and must be regarded in a certain aspect as something absolute. The practice of every-day life, as well as jurisprudence, which closely adheres for the most part to the notions prevalent in every-day life, distinguish two categories in the wherewithal of traffic—goods which have become money and goods which have not. And the ground of this distinction, we find, lies essentially in that difference in the saleableness of commodities set forth above—a difference so significant for practical life and which comes to be further emphasized by intervention of the state. This distinction, moreover, finds expression in language in the difference of meaning attaching to 'money' and 'wares,' to 'purchase' and 'exchange.' But it also affords the chief explanation of that superiority of the buyer over the seller, which has found manifold consideration, yet has hitherto been left inadequately explained.

VIII. HOW THE PRECIOUS METALS BECAME MONEY.

The commodities, which under given local and time relations are most saleable, have become money among the same nations at different times, and among different nations at the same time, and they are diverse in kind. The reason why the *precious metals* have become the generally current medium of exchange among here and there a nation prior to its appearance in history, and in the sequel among all peoples of advanced economic civilization, is because their saleableness is far and away superior to that of all other commodities, and at the same time because they are found to be specially qualified for the concomitant and subsidiary functions of money.

There is no centre of population, which has not in the very beginnings of civilization come keenly to desire and eagerly to covet the precious metals, in primitive times for their utility and [253] peculiar beauty as in themselves ornamental, subsequently as the choicest materials for plastic and architectural decoration, and especially for ornaments and vessels of every kind. In spite of their natural scarcity, they are well distributed geographically, and, in proportion to most other metals, are easy to extract and elaborate. Further, the ratio of the available quantity of the precious metals to the total requirement is so small, that the number of those whose need of them is unsupplied, or at least insufficiently supplied, together with the extent of this unsupplied need, is always relatively large—larger more or less than in the case of other more important, though more abundantly available, commodities. Again, the class of persons who wish to acquire the precious metals, is, by reason of the kind of wants which by these are satisfied, such as quite specially to include those members of the community who can most efficaciously barter; and thus the desire for the precious metals is as a rule more effective. Nevertheless, the limits of the effective desire for the precious metals extend also to those strata of the population who can less effectively barter, by reason of the great divisibility of the precious metals, and the enjoyment procured by the expenditure of even very small quantities of them in individual economy. Besides this there are the wide limits in time and space of the saleableness of the precious metals; a consequence, on the one hand, of the almost unlimited distribution in space of the need of them, together with their low cost of transport as compared with their value, and, on the other hand, of their unlimited durability and the relatively slight cost of hoarding them. In no national economy which has advanced beyond the first stages of development are there any commodities, the saleableness of which is so little restricted in such a number of respects— personally, quantitatively, spatially, and temporally—as the precious metals. It cannot be doubted that, long before they had become the generally acknowledged media of exchange, they were, amongst very many peoples, meeting a positive and effective demand at all times and places, and practically in any quantity that found its way to market.

Hence arose a circumstance, which necessarily became of special import for their becoming money. For anyone under those conditions, having any of the precious metals at his disposal, there was not only the reasonable prospect of his being able to convert them in all markets at any time and practically in all quantities, but also—and this is after all the criterion of saleableness—the prospect of converting them at prices corresponding at [254] any time to the general economic situation, *at economic prices.* The proportionately strong, persistent, and omnipresent desire on the part of the most effective bargainers has gone farther to exclude prices of the moment, of emergency, of accident, in the case of the precious metals, than in the case of any other goods whatever, especially since these, by reason of their costliness, durability, and easy preservation, had become the most popular vehicle for hoarding as well as the goods most highly favoured in commerce.

Under such circumstances it became the leading idea in the minds of the more intelligent bargainers, and then, as the situation came to be more generally understood, in the mind of every one, that the stock of goods destined to be exchanged for other goods must in the first instance be laid out in precious metals, or must be converted into them, even if the agent in question did not directly need them, or had already supplied his wants in that direction. But in and by this function, the precious metals are already constituted generally current media of exchange. In other words, they hereby function as commodities for which everyone seeks to exchange his market-goods, not, as a rule, in order to consumption but entirely because of their special saleableness, in the intention of exchanging them subsequently for other goods directly profitable to him. No accident, no the consequence of state compulsion, nor voluntary convention of traders effected this. It was the just apprehending of their individual self-interest which brought it to pass, that all the more economically advanced nations accepted the precious metals as money as soon as a sufficient supply of them had been collected and introduced into commerce. The advance from less to more costly money-stuffs depends upon analogous causes.

This development was materially helped forward by the ratio of exchange between the precious metals and other commodities undergoing smaller fluctuations, more or less, than that existing between most other goods,—a stability which is due to the peculiar circumstances attending the production, consumption, and exchange of the precious metals, and is thus connected with the so-called intrinsic grounds determining their exchange value. It constitutes yet another reason why each man, in the first instance (*i.e.* till he invests in goods directly useful to him), should lay in his available exchange-stock in precious metals, or convert it into the latter. Moreover the *homogeneity* of the precious metals, and the consequent facility with which they can serve as *res fungibiles* in relations of obligation, have led to forms of contract [255] by which traffic has been rendered more easy; this too has materially promoted the saleableness of the precious metals, and thereby their adoption as money. Finally the precious metals, in consequence of the peculiarity of their *colour*, their *ring*, and partly also of their *specific gravity*, are with some practice not difficult to recognize, and through their taking a durable stamp can be easily controlled as to quality and weight; this too has materially contributed to raise their saleableness and to forward the adoption and diffusion of them as money.

IX. Influence of the Sovereign Power.

Money has not been generated by law. In its origin it is a social, and not a state-institution. Sanction by the authority of the state is a notion alien to it. On the other hand, however, by state recognition and state regulation, this social institution of money has been perfected and adjusted to the manifold and varying needs of an evolving commerce, just as customary rights have been perfected and adjusted by statute law. Treated originally by weight, like other commodities, the precious metals have by degrees attained as coins a shape by which their intrinsically high saleableness has experienced a material increase. The fixing of a coinage so as to include all grades of value (*Wertstufen*), and the establishment and maintenance of coined pieces so as to win public confidence and, as far as is possible, to forestall risk concerning their genuineness, weight, and fineness, and above all the ensuring their circulation in general, have been everywhere recognized as important functions of state administration.

The difficulties experienced in the commerce and modes of payment of any country from the competing action of the several commodities serving as currency, and further the circumstance, that concurrent standards induce a manifold insecurity in trade, and render necessary various conversions of the circulating media, have led to the legal recognition of certain commodities as money (to legal standards). And where more than one commodity has been acquiesced in, or admitted, as the legal form of payment, law or some system of appraisement has fixed a definite ratio of value amongst them.

All these measures nevertheless have not first made money of the precious metals, but have only perfected them in their function as money.

CARL MENGER.
Translated by CAROLINE A. FOLEY, M.A.

Made in United States
North Haven, CT
08 April 2024